THIS HALLOWEEN ACTIVITY BOOK

belongs to ___________________

WHICH TWO ARE THE SAME?

Circle the two that are the same in each row

TRACING LINES

Follow the paths with your pencil

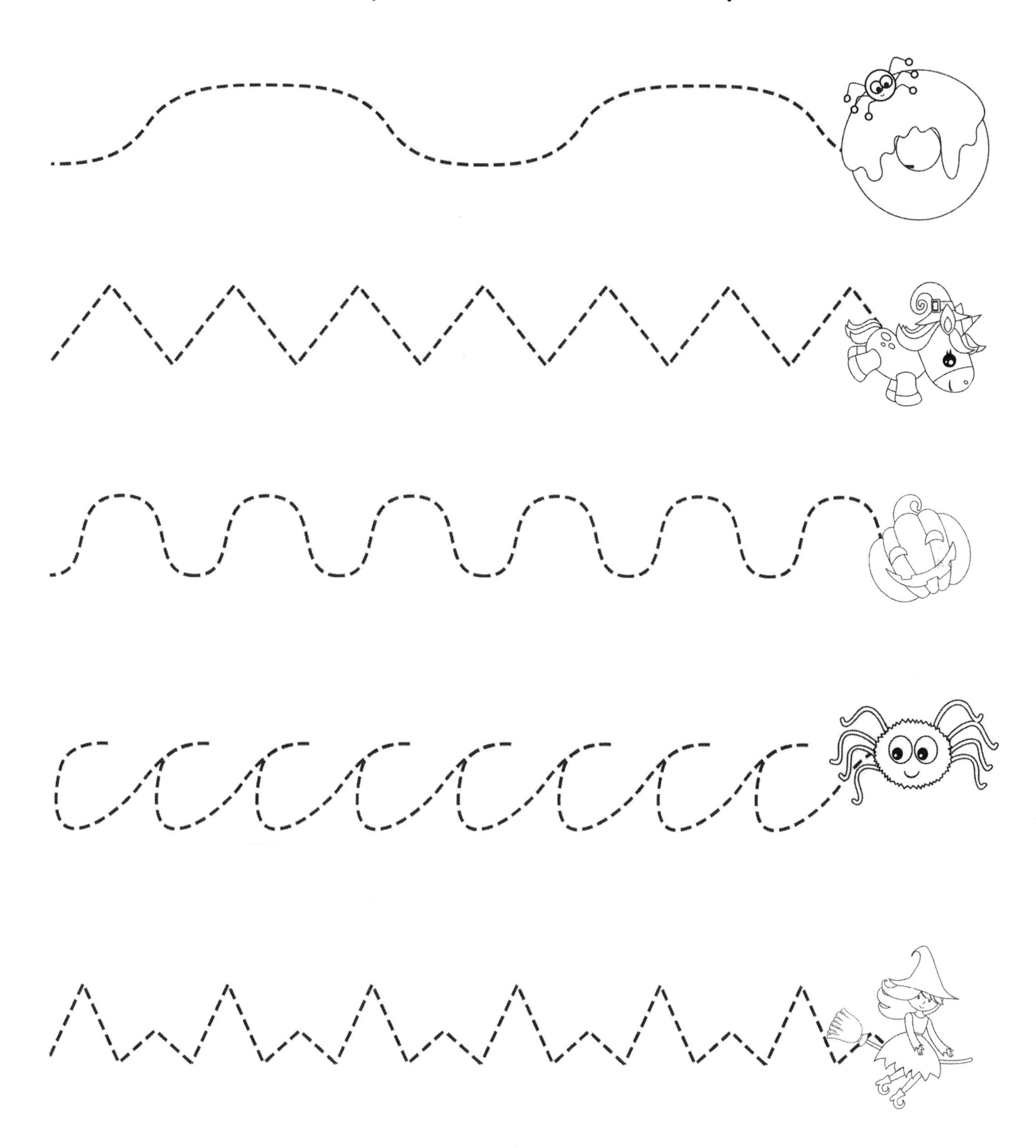

SPOT THE DIFFERENCES

Circle what is different in the two pictures

DRAW YOUR COSTUME!

WHAT COMES NEXT?

Draw what comes next in each Halloween pattern

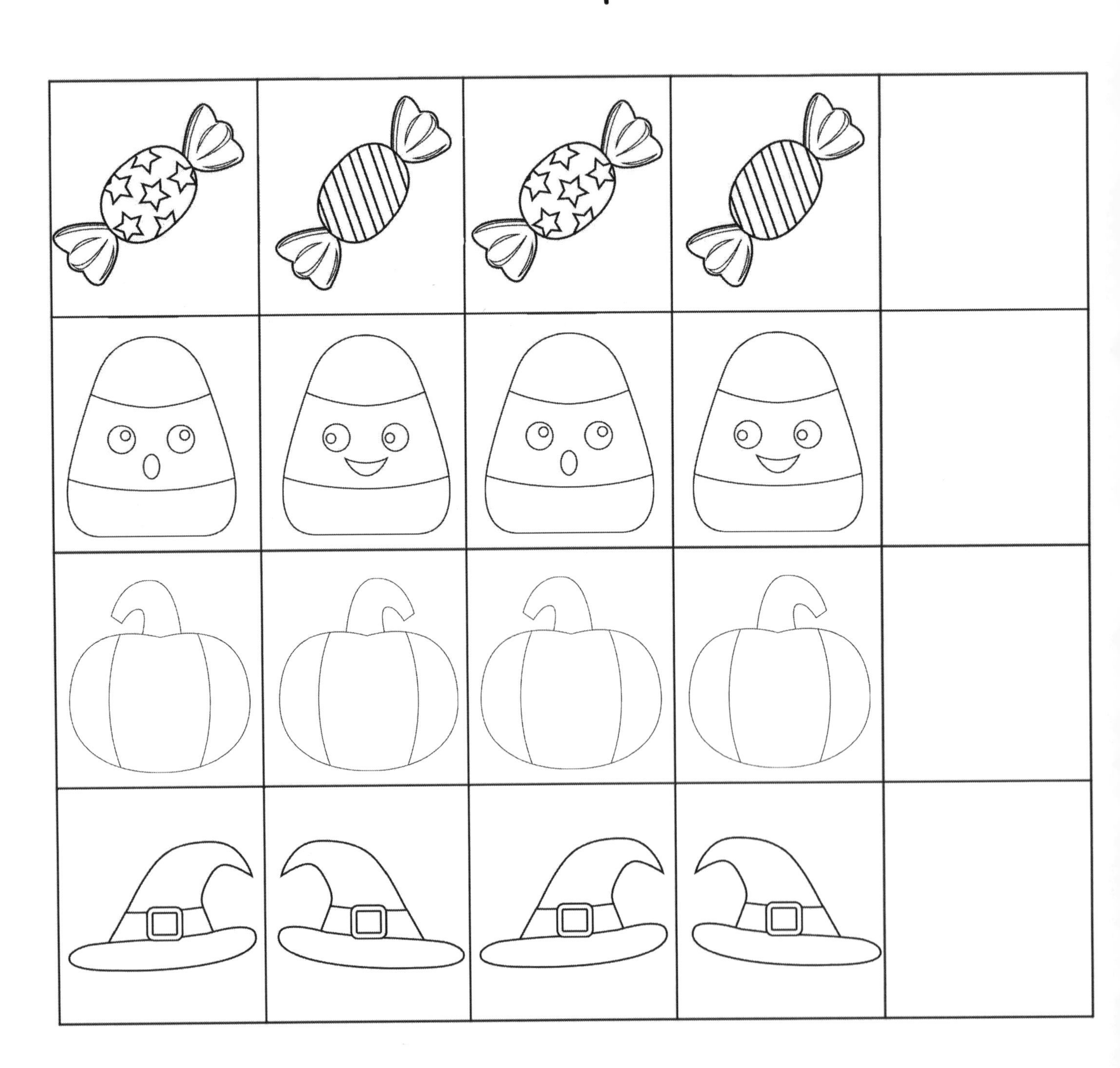

FINISH THE DRAWING

Draw a mirror image of what's on the page

HOW MANY?

Add up how many of each thing can you see

MISSING LINES

Finish the missing lines to complete the drawing of this smiling witch

CIRCLE THE ODD ONE OUT

The answer changes depending on
your reasons!

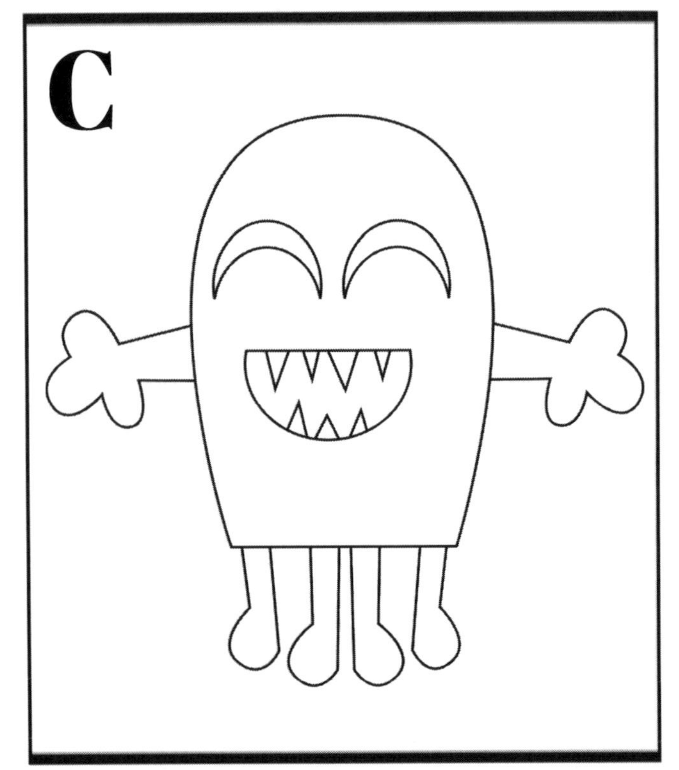

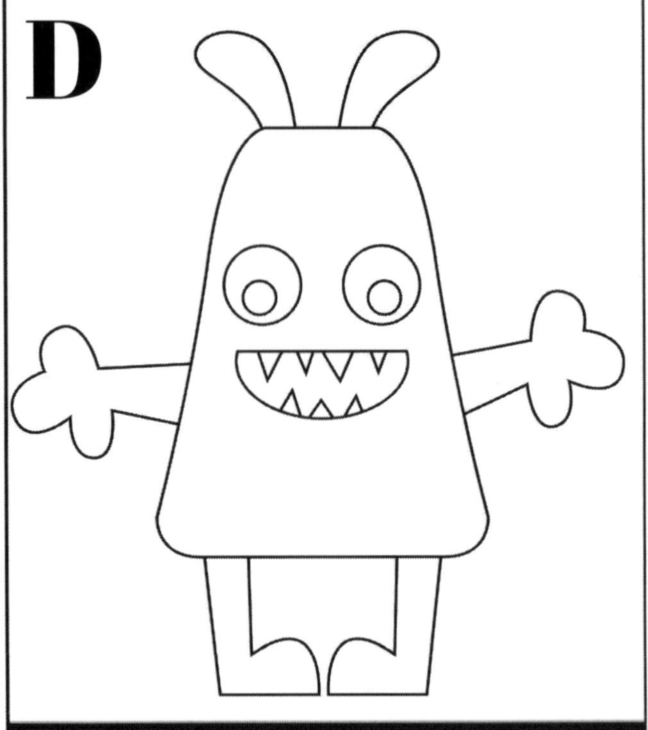

GRID DRAWING

Use the grid to help you draw the happy bat!

A-MAZE-ING FUN

HALLOWEEN TIC-TAC-TOE

Use spiders and pumpkins instead of Xs and Os

DOT-TO-DOT PICTURE

Starting at number one, join the dots until something appears. Then color it in!

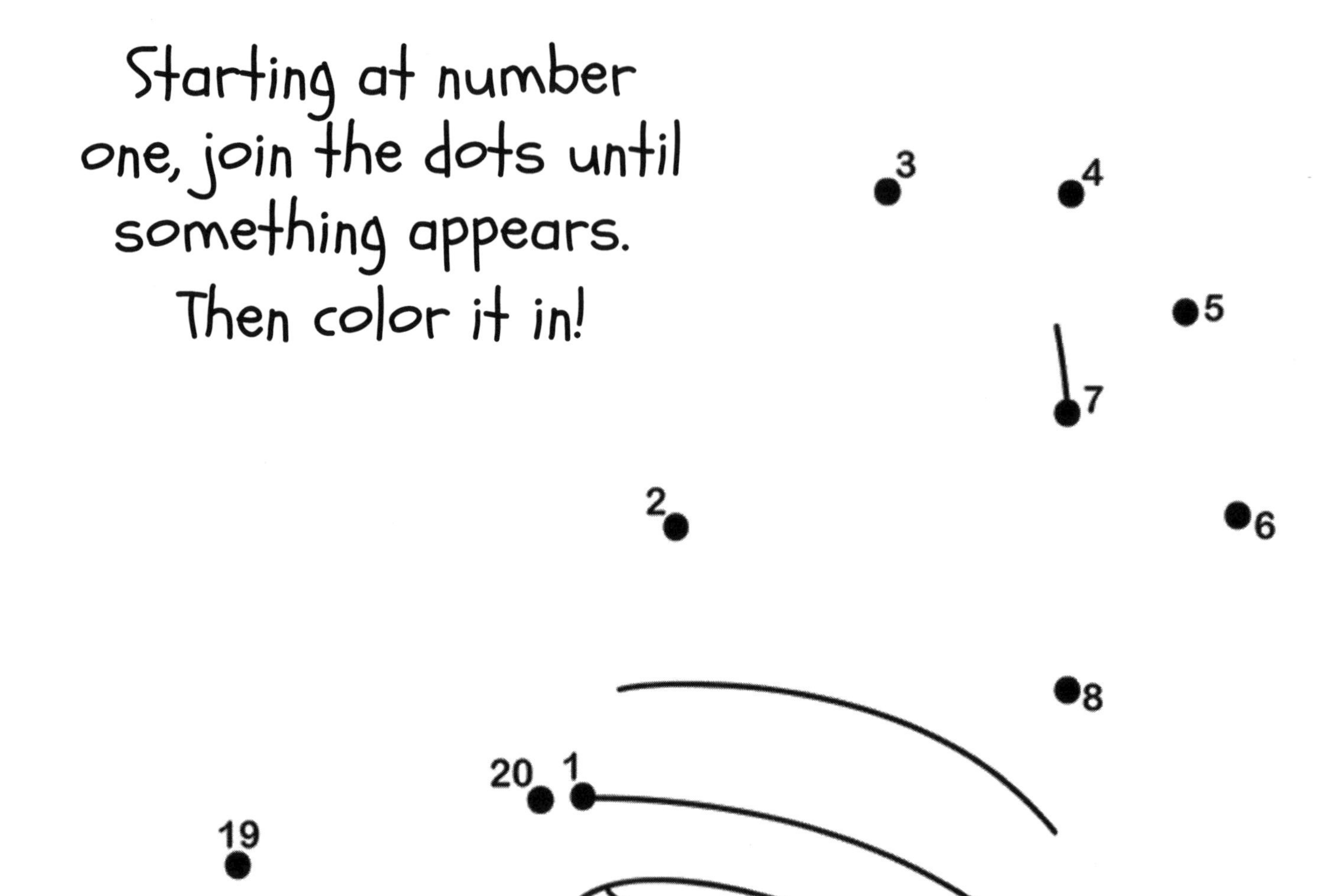

FINISH THE DRAWING

Draw a mirror image of what's on the page

A-MAZE-ING FUN

Help the witch find her cat

BE A WITCH
Draw your
own face!

SPOT THE DIFFERENCES

Circle what is different in the two pictures

DOT-TO-DOT PICTURE

Starting at number one, join the dots until something appears.

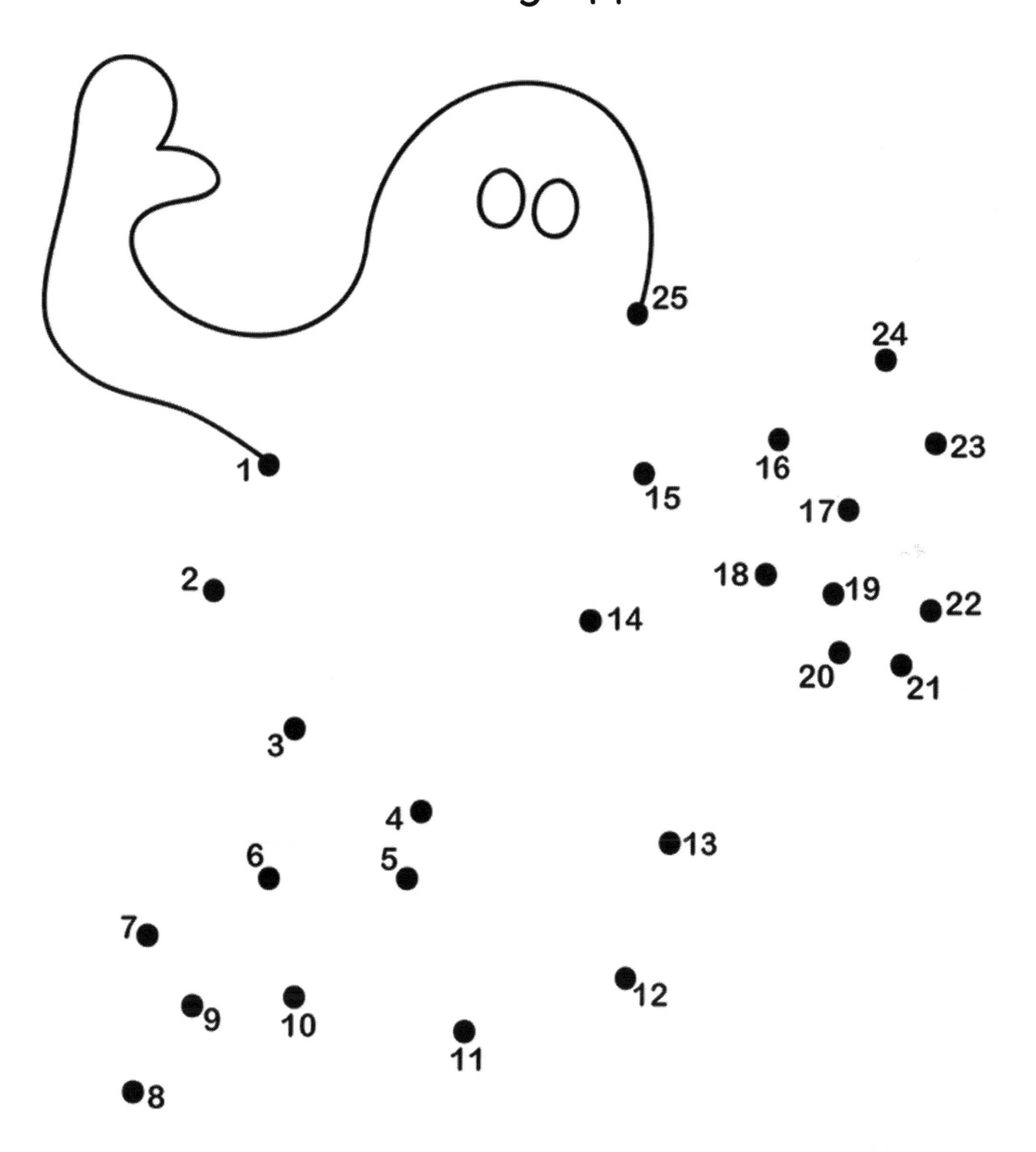

DRAW A FACE ON THE BAT

GRID DRAWING

Use the grid to help you draw the happy bat!

WHAT KIND OF WITCH BELONGS TO THESE FEET?

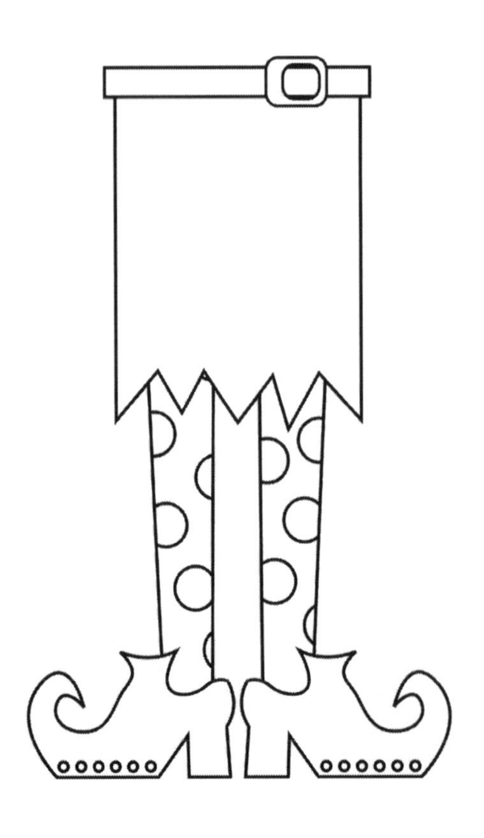

DOT-TO-DOT PICTURE

Starting at number one, join the dots until something appears. Then color it in!

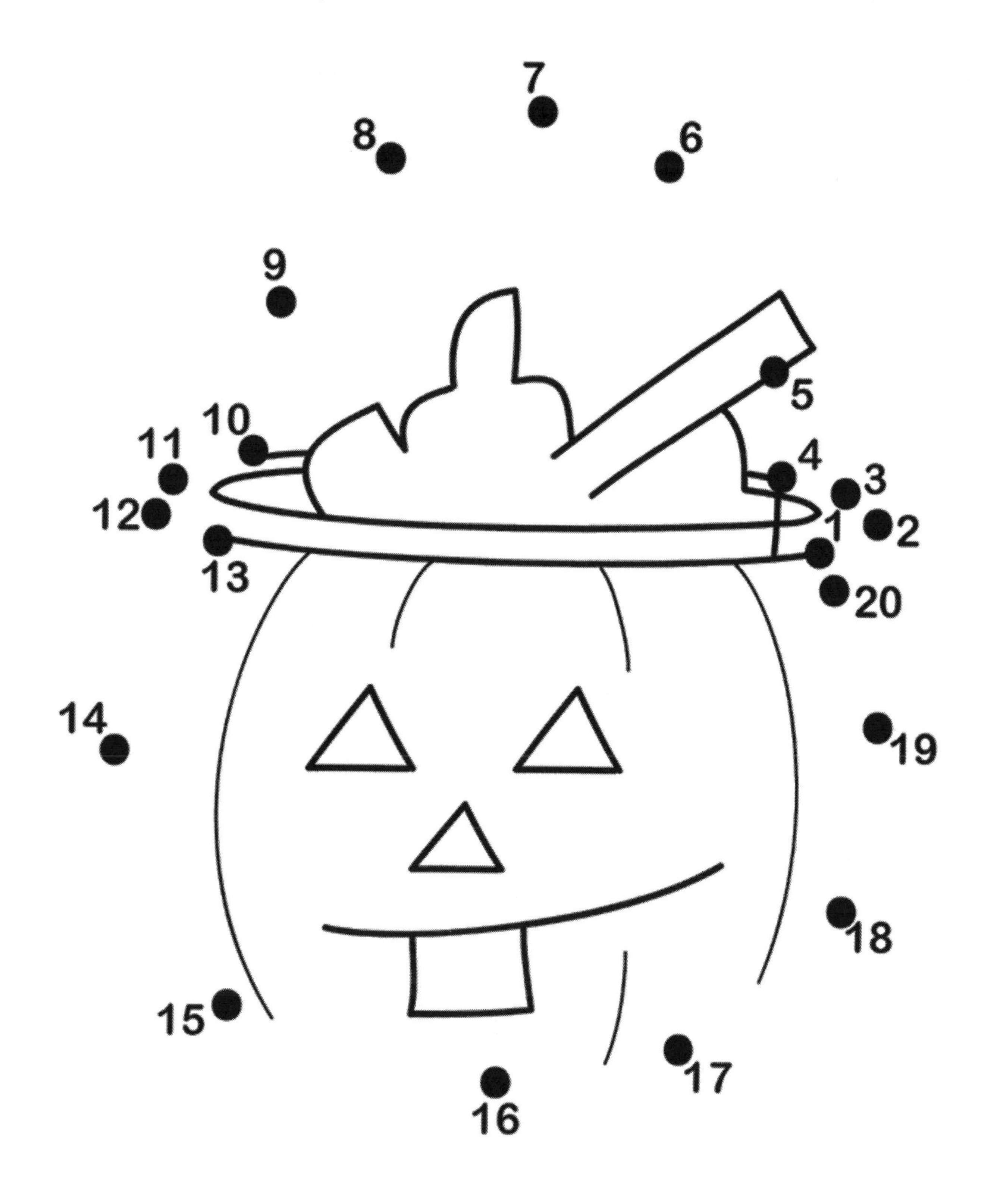

FINISH THE DRAWING

Draw a mirror image of what's on the page

A-MAZE-ING FUN

The mummy needs to finish decorating his Jack O'Lantern, but where is it? Help him find it!

FRANKEN-WHO?

Draw yourself or a friend as Frankenstein

The following pages have no instructions on them, and they only have pictures to color in on one side. This is so you can cut out the pages to display them or send them to friends and family who would love to see your artwork.

Happy coloring!

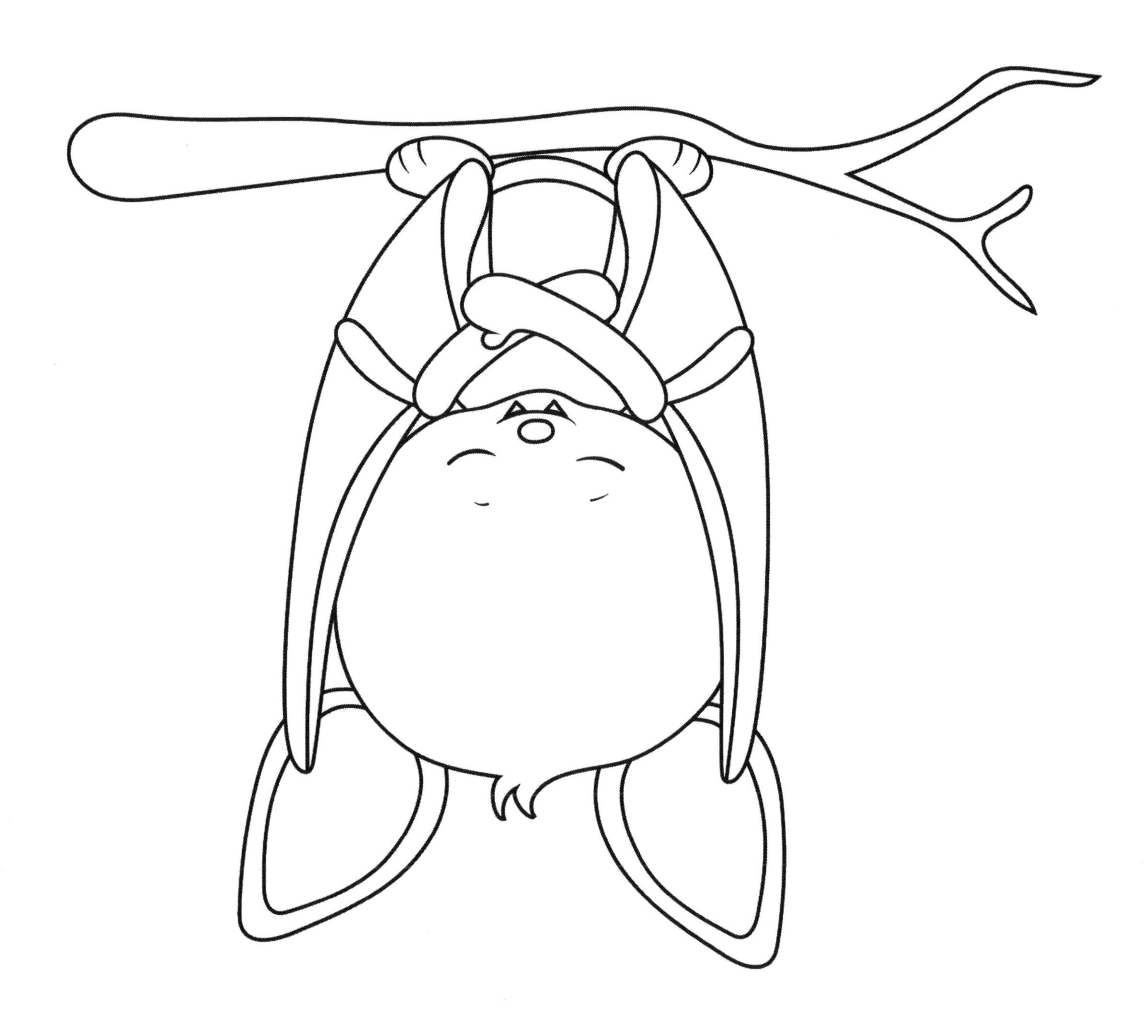

SOLUTIONS

WHICH TWO ARE THE SAME?

Circle the two that are the same in each row

SPOT THE DIFFERENCES

Circle what is different in the two pictures

WHAT COMES NEXT?

Draw what comes next in each Halloween pattern

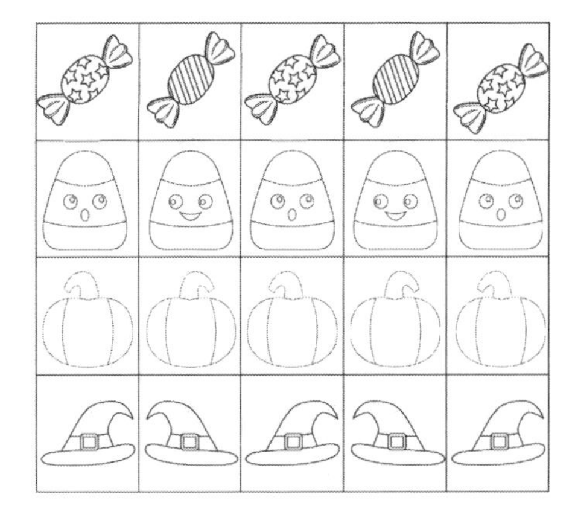

HOW MANY?

Add up how many of each thing can you see

CIRCLE THE ODD ONE OUT

Monster A is the only one with fuzzy hair
Monster B is the only one with a nose, with only 2 teeth; the only square shaped monster;
Monster C is the only one with 4 legs, no ears; with crescent-shaped eyes;
Monster D is the only one with turned in feet.

A-MAZE-ING MAZE

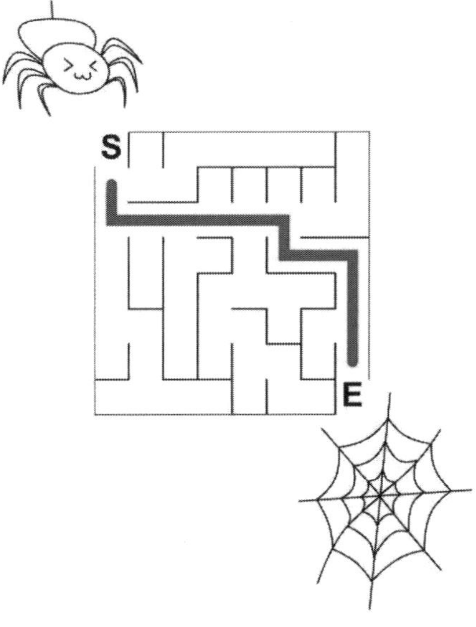

A-MAZE-ING MAZE

SPOT THE DIFFERENCES

Circle what is different in the two pictures

A-MAZE-ING MAZE

Made in the USA
Middletown, DE
19 September 2023

38798331R00029